# The Best of
# Christmas

May there come
to you
at this Holiday Time
an abundance
of the precious things
of Life;
Health, Happiness
and Enduring Friendships

a. Lincoln

## ideals®

Ideals Publishing Corp.
Nashville, Tennessee

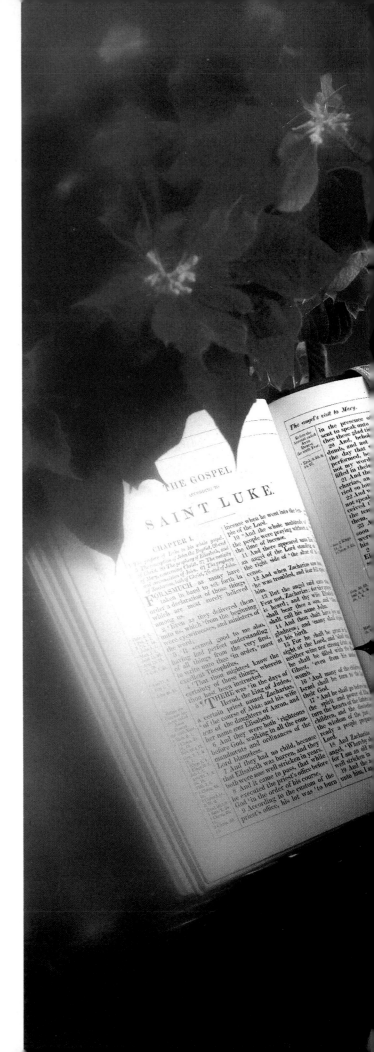

# The Best of
# *Christmas*

## ACKNOWLEDGMENTS

MEMORIES OF A COUNTRY CHRISTMAS by Hazel Andrews. Reprinted by permission from *Modern Maturity*. Copyright 1971 by the American Association of Retired Persons; O TO BE IN IOWA from *JULIA HARRINGTON* by Richard Bissell, copyright © 1969 by Richard Bissell. By permission of Little, Brown and Company; AT CHRISTMASTIME by Camilla R. Bittle. Reprinted by permission of *Woman's Day Magazine*. Copyright © 1962 by CBS Publications, Inc. Reprinted by permission of Brandt & Brandt Literary Agents, Inc.; A TIME FOR GIVING by Jill Briscoe from her book, *A TIME FOR GIVING*. Copyright © 1979 by Jill Briscoe. Reprinted by permission of Briscoe Ministries; IT'S GETTING TO BE CHRISTMAS by Beverly Butler. Copyright © 1974 by Beverly Butler. Reprinted by permission of Larry Sternig Literary Agency; MY CHRISTMAS MIRACLE by Taylor Caldwell. Copyright © 1961 by Taylor Caldwell. Reprinted by permission of The William Morris Agency, Inc. on behalf of the author; SKATERS AT DUSK from *THE CRYSTAL FOUNTAIN* by Grace Noll Crowell. Copyright 1948 by Harper & Row, Publishers, Inc. Reprinted by permission of Harper & Row, Publishers, Inc.; IN THE WEEK WHEN CHRISTMASTIME COMES from *ELEANOR FARJEON'S POEMS FOR CHILDREN* (J.B. Lippincott). Copyright 1927, renewed 1955 by Eleanor Farjeon. Reprinted by permission of Harper & Row, Publishers, Inc.; THE DUEL from *POEMS OF CHILDHOOD* by Eugene Field (Charles Scribner's Sons); STOPPING BY WOODS ON A SNOWY EVENING from *THE POETRY OF ROBERT FROST*, edited by Edward Connery Lathem. Copyright 1923, © 1969 by Holt, Rinehart and Winston. Copyright 1951 by Robert Frost. Reprinted by permission of Henry Holt and Company; excerpt from LET'S KEEP CHRISTMAS by Peter Marshall, copyright © 1952, 1953 by Catherine Marshall, renewed 1981. Published by Chosen Books, Fleming H. Revell Company. Used by permission; THE BALLAD OF BEFANA by Phyllis McGinley. Reprinted by permission of Curtis Brown, Ltd., copyright © 1958 by Phyllis McGinley; SPECIAL STARLIGHT from *THE COMPLETE POEMS OF CARL SANDBURG*, copyright © 1950 by Carl Sandburg, renewed 1978 by Margaret Sandburg, Helga Sandburg Crile, and Janet Sandburg. Reprinted by permission of Harcourt Brace Jovanovich, Inc.; FESTIVE DECEMBER by Gladys Taber. Copyright 1977, The Family Circle, Inc. Reprinted by permission of Brandt & Brandt Literary Agents, Inc. Our sincere thanks to the following whose addresses we were unable to locate: Louise A. Baldwin for ON THE DAY THAT FOLLOWS CHRISTMAS; the Estate of Mildred H. Bell for BRINGING HOME THE TREE; Robert Freeman Bound for THE FIRST SNOW; Vincent Godfrey Burns for THE MIRACLE OF CHRISTMAS; Grace E. Easley for CHRISTMAS CARDS; Nellie Varnes Fultz for THE SWEET SOUNDS CHRISTMAS BRINGS; Esther Lloyd Hagg for IT WAS NOT STRANGE; Gertrude Bryson Holman for THERE'S CHRISTMAS IN THE AIR; Fairy Walker Lane for CHRISTMAS WREATH; The Estate of Alice Leedy Mason for A CHRISTMAS PUP, A CHRISTMAS KITTEN, and FLIGHT INTO EGYPT; the Estate of Denis McCarthy for CHRISTMAS LEGENDS from *THE HARP OF LIFE* by Denis McCarthy, published in 1929 by the Carrolton Publishing Company, Boston; Estelle Ellington Platt for THE WONDER OF CHRISTMAS; Isabel Shaw for CHRISTMAS CHANT; and Timothy Traynor for REFLECTIONS AT WINTER TWILIGHT.

# Table of Contents

The Preparations for
*Christmas*

# Bringing Home the Tree

The wooded fields sent out a call,
And when they called to me,
I knew that it was time to go
To find a Christmas tree.

I tracked about in fields of snow
From morn till nearly night,
Where all the dark and barren spots
Were blanketed with white.

At last I found the perfect tree,
A cedar straight and tall.
I brought it home, where it would be
A joy to one and all.

It was the best tree in the world—
The children thought it so.
For such a tree, a hundred times
I'd trample through the snow.

*Mildred Harper Bell*

# The First Snow

From lowering clouds
And a temperature fall,
The first snow of winter
Would come with a squall.

We waited for hours,
As children all will,
After Father had told us
The news with a thrill.

'Twas the oddest sensation
When we'd gaze at the sky;
We seemed to be falling,
But we didn't know why.

Then early that evening
The first flakes descended;
And when we retired,
The fall hadn't ended.

Next morning the light
Reflected from snow
Made shimmering patterns
With walls all aglow.

We looked from our beds
At a white, silent scene
Of tall, pearly trees
And the buildings between.

And our happy, old dog,
With great barking leaps,
Was chasing a rabbit
Through high, snowy heaps.

Oh, the wonderful joy
To be young and know
The thrill of a child
At winter's first snow.

*Robert Freeman Bound*

*Photo opposite
A. Devaney, Inc.*

# "Read to Me"

## The Duel

The gingham dog and the calico cat
Side by side on the table sat.
'Twas half-past twelve, and (what do you think!)
Not one nor t'other had slept a wink!
The old Dutch clock and the Chinese plate
Appeared to know as sure as fate
There was going to be a terrible spat.
*(I wasn't there; I simply state*
*What was told to me by the Chinese plate!)*


The gingham dog went, "Bow-wow-wow!"
And the calico cat replied, "Mee-ow!"
The air was littered, an hour or so,
With bits of gingham and calico,
While the old Dutch clock in the chimney place
Up with its hands before its face,
For it always dreaded a family row!
*(Now mind, I'm only telling you*
*What the old Dutch clock declares is true!)*


The Chinese plate looked very blue,
And wailed, "Oh, dear! What shall we do!"
But the gingham dog and the calico cat
Wallowed this way and tumbled that,
Employing every tooth and claw
In the awfullest way you ever saw.
And, oh! how the gingham and calico flew!
*(Don't fancy I exaggerate . . .*
*I got my news from the Chinese plate!)*

Next morning, where the two had sat
They found no trace of dog or cat;
And some folks think unto this day
That burglars stole the pair away!
But the truth about the cat and pup
Is this: They ate each other up!
Now, what do you really think of that!
*(The old Dutch clock, it told me so,*
*And that is how I came to know.)*

Eugene Field

# Everywhere...The Christmas Spirit

Green palm fronds and sandy beaches,
Golden glow of sun above,
Red poinsettias in each garden,
Faces warm with joy and love.

Christmas carols softly playing,
Kisses beneath mistletoe;
Yuletide in the heart of Dixie—
Who could feel a need for snow?

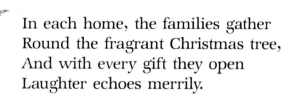

In each home, the families gather
Round the fragrant Christmas tree,
And with every gift they open
Laughter echoes merrily.

Blest by such a glad reunion,
Christmas spirit, we have found,
Flourishes in any setting
Where true love and faith abound.

D. A. Hoover

*Photo opposite*
*Bruce Coleman, Inc.*

# Let's Keep Christmas

I thank God for Christmas,
Would that it lasted all year.
For on Christmas Eve and Christmas Day, all the
world is a better place,
    and men and women are more lovable.
Love itself seeps into every heart, and miracles
happen.

When Christmas doesn't make your heart swell up
until it nearly bursts . . .
    and fill your eyes with tears . . .
      and make you all soft and warm inside . . .
then you'll know that something inside of you is dead.

We hope that there will be snow for Christmas.
Why?
It is not really important, but it is so nice, and
old-fashioned, and appropriate, we think.

Isn't it wonderful to think that nothing can *really
harm* the joy of Christmas . . .
Although your Christmas tree decorations will
include many new gadgets, such as lights with
bubbles in them, it's the old tree decorations that
mean the most, the ones you save carefully from
year to year . . .
    the crooked star that goes on the top of the tree . . .
      the ornaments that you've been so careful with.

And you'll bring out the tiny manger
    and the shed
    and the little figures of the Holy Family,
and lovingly arrange them on the mantel
    or in the middle of the dining room table.

And getting the tree will be a family event, with
great excitement for the children;
And there will be a closet into which you'll forbid
your husband to look.
And he will be moving through the house
mysteriously with bundles under his coat,
    and you'll pretend not to notice.

There will be the fragrance of cookies baking,
    spices and fruitcake . . .
and the warmth of the house shall be melodious
with the lilting strains of "Silent Night, Holy
Night."
And you'll listen to the wonderful Christmas music
on the radio,
Some of the songs will be modern—good enough
music perhaps—but it will be the old carols,
    the lovely old Christmas hymns that will mean
the most.

And forests of fir trees will march right into our
living rooms.
There will be bells on our doors
    and holly wreaths in our windows,
and we shall sweep the Noel skies for their
brightest colors and festoon our homes with stars.
There will be a chubby stocking hung by the
fireplace,
    and with finger to lip, you will whisper
and ask me to tiptoe, for a little tousled head is
asleep and must not be awakened
    until after Santa has come.

And finally, Christmas morning will come.
Don't worry—you'll be ready for it—
    You'll catch the spirit all right,
or *it will catch you, which is even better.*
And then you will remember what Christmas
means . . . the beginning of Christianity . . .
    the second chance for the world . . .
        the hope for peace . . .
            and the only way.
The promise that the angels sang is the most
wonderful music the world has ever heard:
    "Peace on earth and goodwill toward men."

*Peter Marshall*

# Christmas Cookies

## Choco-Cherry Flags

Yield: about 8 dozen

1 cup (6-ounce package) semi-sweet chocolate chips
1 cup butter *or* margarine, softened
1½ cups sugar
1 egg
1 teaspoon vanilla

2½ cups unsifted all-purpose flour
1½ teaspoons baking powder
½ teaspoon salt
⅓ cup chopped, red candied cherries
½ teaspoon almond extract

Melt chocolate chips in the top of a double boiler over hot (not boiling) water. Cream butter *or* margarine and sugar in large mixer bowl until light and fluffy. Add egg and vanilla; beat well. In a separate bowl, combine flour, baking powder and salt; gradually add to creamed mixture. Beat well. Divide dough into thirds. Combine one-third of the dough with candied cherries and almond extract; blend well. Add melted chocolate to remaining two-thirds dough; blend well. Line a 9 x 5-inch loaf pan with waxed paper. Press half of the chocolate dough firmly into prepared pan. Press cherry dough on top of chocolate dough. Press remaining chocolate dough on top. Cover pan tightly; chill several hours or overnight. Carefully remove dough from pan by pulling on edges of waxed paper. Cut dough in half lengthwise. Slice each half into 1/4-inch thick slices. Place on an ungreased cookie sheet. Bake at 400° for 8 to 10 minutes or until almost set. Cool slightly on cookie sheet. Remove from cookie sheet; cool on wire rack.

## Pinwheel Cookies

Yield: about 3 dozen

½ cup butter *or* margarine, softened
1 package (3 ounces) cream cheese, softened
1 cup sugar
1 egg
1 teaspoon vanilla

2¼ cups unsifted all-purpose flour, divided
½ teaspoon baking powder
½ teaspoon salt
⅛ teaspoon baking soda
½ cup cocoa

Cream butter *or* margarine, cream cheese, sugar, egg and vanilla in large mixer bowl until light and fluffy. In a separate bowl, combine 1½ cups of the flour, baking powder, salt and baking soda; blend into creamed mixture. Divide dough in half. Add cocoa to one half of dough; blend well. Add ¾ cup flour to remaining half of dough; blend well. Roll each half into a 9-inch square. (If dough is too soft, chill about 15 minutes.) Place chocolate dough on top of vanilla. Roll up jelly-roll style. Wrap tightly in waxed paper; chill several hours or overnight. Slice dough ¼ inch thick. Place on an ungreased cookie sheet. Bake at 350° for 12 to 15 minutes or until lightly browned. Remove from cookie sheet; cool on wire rack.

# The Decorations of
# *Christmas*

# Christmas Wreath

Decorate a Christmas window,
Holly wreath with berries red;
Bring a thrill of Yuletide pleasure
To the folks who homeward tread.

Light them on their homeward journey,
Renewed with joy through the night;
Yours may be the kindly message
That will make their Christmas bright.

*Fairy Walker Lane*

# The Miracle of Christmas

The miracle of Christmas
  Is a wreath upon the door,
A Christmas tree in splendor
  With gifts spread upon the floor,
A warm and glowing fire
  In a cozy fireplace,
And happy, cheerful people
  With a smile on every face.

The miracle of Christmas
  Is a star-filled winter night
With window after window
  Aglow with candlelight,
With patterns of purple shadows
  Along the gleaming snow,
With happy youthful voices
  Singing carols as they go.

The miracle of Christmas
  Is a babe of long ago
And a gentle mother kneeling
  By a manger crude and low
And one star of glory shining
  In the heavens up above
For the One who is the symbol
  Of God's everlasting love.

*Vincent Godfrey Burns*

*Photo opposite*
*Winston Pote*

# Special Starlight

The creator of night and of birth
was the maker of the stars.

Shall we look up now at stars in winter
And call them always sweeter friends
Because this story of a mother and a child
Never is told with the stars left out?

Is it a holy night now when a child issues
Out of the dark and the unknown
Into the starlight?

Down a winter evening sky,
when a woman hovers
between two great doorways,
between entry and exit,
between pain to be laughed at,
joy to be wept over—
do the silver-white lines
then come from holy stars?
Shall the newcomer, the newborn,
be given soft flannels,
swaddling-cloths called holy?

Shall all wanderers over the earth, all
homeless ones,
All against whom doors are shut and
words spoken—
Shall these find the earth less strange tonight?
Shall they hear news, a whisper on the
night wind?
"A child is born." "The meek shall inherit
the earth."
"And they crucified him . . . they spat upon
him."
"And he rose from the dead."

Shall a quiet dome of stars high over
Make signs and a friendly language
Among all nations?

Shall they yet gather with no clenched fists
    at all,
And look into each other's faces and see eye
    to eye,
And find ever new testaments of man as a
    sojourner
And a toiler and a brother of fresh under-
    standings?

> Shall there be now always
> believers and more believers
> of sunset and moonrise,
> of moonset and dawn,
> of wheeling numbers of stars,
> and wheels within wheels?

Shall plain habitations off the well-known
    roads
Count now for a little more than they used
    to?

Shall plain ways and people held close to
    earth
Be reckoned among things to be written
    about?

Shall tumult, grandeur, fanfare, panoply,
    prepared loud noises
Stand equal to a quiet heart, thoughts, vast
    dreams
Of men conquering the earth by con-
    quering themselves?
Is there a time for ancient genius of man
To be set for comparison with the latest
    generations?
Is there a time for stripping to simple,
    childish questions?

> On a holy night we may say:
> The creator of night and of birth
> was the maker of the stars.

*Carl Sandburg*

# Our Snowman

We rolled a large snowball
All over the ground;
To gather up snowflakes
We pushed it around.
And as it went rolling,
It grew and it grew;
Then we made another
So there would be two.

It was really hard work;
I called for my mother
To help put the second
On top of the other.
Then a smaller one yet
Was used for a head,
And we gave him a hat
And a muffler of red.

When his plump, snowy arms
Were in the right place,
We looked for some felt
To mark out his face.
A mouth which was easy,
Two eyes, and a nose,
The rest was for buttons
To trim up his clothes.

We turned his mouth upward
To give him a smile,
And hoped we could keep him
At least for awhile.
He looked very handsome
When he was all done,
And we let him stand guard
With a broom for a gun.

*Harriet Whipple*

*Photo opposite*
*Freelance Photographers Guild*

# Country Christmas

Red hills are trimmed with silver lace,
For Christmastime is near;
Smoke spirals from each fireplace
And glowing logs add cheer.

From the old white church, carols flow
Across the frosted air,
Exalting Christ, born long ago
In a stable bare.

The long Blue Ridge is capped in white,
Pines edge each country mile.
Folks wear, when Christmas is in sight,
A holly-berry smile!

*Earle J. Grant*

# The Story of the Holly Sprig

## By Arthur Upson

"I'd be the shiniest green,"
   Wished once a sprig of holly,
"That e'er at Yule was seen,
   And deck some banquet jolly!"

"I'd be the cheeriest red,"
   Wished once the holly berry,
"That e'er at board rich spread
   Helped make the feasters merry!"

The life within them heard
   Down dark and silent courses,
For each wish is a word
   To those fair-hidden sources.

All summer in the wood,
   While they were riper growing,
The deep roots understood,
   And helped without their knowing.

In a little market stall
   At Yule the sprig lay waiting,
For fine folk one and all
   Passed by that open grating.

The eve of Christmas Day
   It had been passed by many,
When one turned not away
   And bought it for a penny.

Hers was a home of care
   Which not a wreath made jolly;
The only Christmas there
   Was that sweet sprig of holly.

"Oh, this is better far
   Than banquet!" thought the berry;
The leaves glowed like a star
   And made that cottage merry!

# At Christmastime

At Christmastime when I was small,
  We placed the figure in the stall
(Mary, blessed Babe, and all),
  Hung mistletoe high in the hall,
Made calendars for kitchen walls,
  And decked our tree with shiny balls.


On Christmas Eve beside the fire,
  We gathered round the wicker chair
To hear our mother's mother read
  Of sugarplums that danced in air,
Of moonlight on new-fallen snow;
  And this we knew—as children know—
Was evidence of love below
  The great high arc of heaven's dome,
Of Christmases secured by home.


The cold—a stabbing, piercing knife,
  The stars—small, dazzling flecks of light,
Our breath rose up in columns white,
  And, oh, the still of Christmas night!


Each year we did the very same,
  Wrote cards, made lists, our cousins came.
On Christmas Eve out caroling,
  Our cheeks, bared to the icy sting
Of snowy wind, grew tingling.
  We sang as loud as we could sing.


I ask myself—what did it mean,
  The stockings, tinsel, branches green,
The smell of oranges and pie,
  The wreaths, the bells, the winter sky
Where once a star shone for the child,
  Whose birth we hailed with praises mild
While overhead the Milky Way
  Was passage for old Santa's sleigh.

We still hang up the mistletoe.
　My children's faces rosy grow,
Their boots squeak on the hard-packed snow.
　Their eyes with eagerness will glow,
And I'm the only one who'll know
　That it was different long ago.


The tree still flaunts its branches.
　The sky is jet; the stars wink light.
There is a hush to Christmas night.
　The songs are still sung out with might
And Santa's toys, a dazzling sight.


The only thing that's changed is me.
　It's not a fir with lights I see,
For only God can make a tree—
　This is what I see.
And children's eyes can only be
　Small windows on eternity.


And so with gifts, and cousins small,
　And so with garlands in the hall,
And firelight's shadows on the wall—
　God's handiwork, that's all.


Yet in this season of our joy
　There are still those who feel a toy
Is all that matters—not the boy
　Whose praises we should all employ,
Lest man all brotherhood destroy.


Come, take your stand; decry the whim
　That turkeys, gifts and greetings slim
Define the core—they are the rim
　And but the glossy surface skim,
For in our hearts we kneel to Him.

*Camilla R. Bittle*

# O Christmas Tree

O Tannenbaum

Translated from the German
English version by RUTH HELLER

GERMAN

*Happily*

1. O Christ-mas tree, O Christ-mas tree, O tree of green, un-
2. O Christ-mas tree, O Christ-mas tree, You set my heart a-
3. O Christ-mas tree, O Christ-mas tree, You come from God, e-
4. O Christ-mas tree, O Christ-mas tree, You speak of God, un-

chang-ing. Your boughs, so green in sum-mer time, Do
sing-ing. Like lit-tle stars, your can-dles bright Send
ter-nal. A sym-bol of the Lord of Love Whom
chang-ing. You tell us all to faith-ful be, And

brave the snow of win-ter-time. O Christ-mas tree, O
to the world a won-drous light. O Christ-mas tree, O
God to man sent from a-bove. O Christ-mas tree, O
trust in God e-ter-nal-ly. O Christ-mas tree, O

Christ-mas tree, O tree of green, un - chang - ing.
Christ-mas tree, You set my heart a - sing - ing.
Christ-mas tree, You come from God, e - ter - nal.
Christ-mas tree, You speak of God, un - chang - ing.

# Deck the Hall

TRADITIONAL

WELSH

*Rollicking*

1. Deck the hall with boughs of hol-ly, Fa la la la la, la la la la.
2. See the blaz-ing Yule be-fore us, Fa la la la la, la la la la.
3. Fast a-way the old year pass-es, Fa la la la la, la la la la.

'Tis the sea-son to be jol-ly, Fa la la la la, la la la la.
Strike the harp and join the cho-rus, Fa la la la la, la la la la.
Hail the new, ye lads and lass-es, Fa la la la la, la la la la.

Don we now our gay ap-par-el, Fa la, la la, la la la,
Fol-low me in mer-ry meas-ure, Fa la, la la, la la la,
Sing we joy-ous all to-geth-er, Fa la, la la, la la la,

Troll the an-cient Yule-tide car-ol, Fa la la la la, la la la la.
While I tell of Yule-tide treas-ure, Fa la la la la, la la la la.
Heed-less of the wind and weath-er, Fa la la la la, la la la la.

# The Sensations of Christmas

# What Is Christmas?

*Christmas is music* . . . the music of carols ringing out in the still night air, the organ, the chimes and the voices of a choir singing "Silent Night, Holy Night."

*Christmas is lights* . . . the candles in our windows, the lighted trees, the eyes of children, and the starlight on a cold December night.

*Christmas is welcome* . . . the wreath on the door, the happiness to answer the doorbell, the warmth of hearts overflowing, "Come in, come in and Merry Christmas."

*Christmas is laughter* . . . the laughter that starts in your toes and bubbles up, the smiles on faces everywhere, the feeling of closeness, of a wonderful secret shared with all mankind.

*Christmas is fragrance* . . . the pine and spruce smell of Christmas trees, the sugary good smell of cookies baking, the spice and raisin smell of fruitcake, the smell of furniture polish, and the cold, crisp smell of outdoors.

*Christmas is giving* . . . the present made by hand, the card picked especially for a certain person, the gift marked "from me to you, with love."

*Carol B. Hayman*

# There's a Song in the Air

There's a song in the air!
There's a star in the sky!
There's a mother's deep prayer
And a baby's low cry!
And the star rains its fire
While the beautiful sing,
For the manger of Bethlehem cradles a King!

There's a tumult of joy
O'er the wonderful birth,
For the Virgin's sweet boy
Is the Lord of the earth.
Ay! the star rains its fire
While the beautiful sing,
For the manger of Bethlehem cradles a King!

We rejoice in the light,
And we echo the song
That comes down through the night
From the heavenly throng.
Ay! we shout to the lovely evangel they bring.
And we greet in his cradle our Savior and King!

*Josiah Gilbert Holland*

*Painting, ANGELS APPEARING TO THE SHEPHERD, Nicholas Berchem*
*(Photo, Three Lions, Inc.)*

# The Sweet Sounds Christmas Brings

They come at first as just a gentle breeze
That rustles leaves still hanging on the trees
And lifts the ones now scattered on the ground,
Dancing a merry, final waltz around.
Then comes a whisper of the fleecy snow—
Of small flakes falling softly to and fro,
A sort of preview of big things to be
When winter gales will festoon every tree.

Soon now you're sure to hear the quail's "bob-white"
Along the hedgerow where he spends the night.
The pheasant's tail sweeps snow before he flies,
His ring-necked beauty mirrored beneath the skies.
Soft on the feeder lands the chickadee,
His chirping notes his humble symphony,
Joined by the junco, cardinal, and jay
Whose mocking noise scares all the rest away.
Out on the snow a rabbit's footprints mark
The paths through fields so barren now and stark.

His ears aloft, his twitching nose spells fear
Of enemies whose presence comes too near;
His sounds too faint unless one bending low
Can hear his heartbeats faint upon the snow.
Now is the time for children's joyous noise—
Of crunching sleds that carry girls and boys,
The click of skates upon the frozen pond
As scores of snowmen guard the banks beyond.

Then come the sounds so sweet at Christmastime,
Bringing again the church bell's measured chime
With old-time carols floating everywhere,
Blended with organ music on the air;
The sound of closing church doors in the night
Revealing streaks of altar candlelight,
The "Merry Christmas" shouts as people leave
And hurry home to joy of Christmas Eve.

Then on the frozen streets the footsteps fall
With awe and magic settling over all.
Now one can fancy hearing angels sing
Their shouts of adoration to the King.
These are the sounds that rival those of spring;
Here reverent thoughts become a quiet thing
Of great abounding peace and hearts applaud
The words, "Be still and know that I am God."

*Nellie Varnes Fultz*

# Hold Fast
# Your Dreams

On Christmas morn I'd love to reach
Into the clear blue skies,
And fill your stocking up with gifts
To make you great and wise.

But most of all, dear boy, I'd like
To leave this gift with you:
Beware of life's synthetic gains
As years go rushing through.

Remember sunsets over fields,
The fish you caught in streams,
Weed out the glitter, gold is cold . . .
Hold fast to all your dreams.

*Annette Victorin*

*Painting opposite
Frances Hook*

# Country Choir Practice

It is on the eve of Christmas,
In the now-forgotten days;
Country church lamps have been lighted,
And its yard is full of sleighs.

Horses tied there to the hitchracks
Now are wearing strands of bells,
Tinkling with their restless movements
To enhance the sound that swells

From the organ in the chapel,
And the carols of the choir.
They practice for tomorrow,
Seated near the blazing fire

Which is roaring now and snapping
In the tall, old Bridge Beach stove,
Stoked with wood chunks brought in autumn
From the nearby woodland grove.

And the picture in the darkness
That the lighted church now makes
Is the kind that leaves impressions
Which no memory forsakes.

It will come in recollection,
Through the years in many ways,
How the country church stood lighted
And its yard was full of sleighs.

*Arthur Thatcher*

# A Child's Face

Christmas is a child's face
Watching from the stair,
Peeking through the banisters
At magic everywhere.

Christmas is a child's face
Rosy, deep with love;
Trusting, like the wise men,
In the star above.

Christmas is a child's face
Shining, soft, and dear;
Believing with such rapture
In a cherished time of year.

Christmas comes in many ways
In many homes apart,
But always it's a child's face
Shining in your heart.

*Virginia Covey Boswell*

*Painting opposite*
*Frances Hook*

# Christmas...Through the Ages

I heard the bells on Christmas Day
Their old, familiar carols play,
    And wild and sweet
    The words repeat
Of peace on earth, goodwill to men!

And thought how, as the day had come
The belfries of all Christendom
    Had rolled along
    The unbroken song
Of peace on earth, goodwill to men!

Till, ringing, singing on its way,
The world revolved from night to day,
    A voice, a chime,
    A chant sublime
Of peace on earth, goodwill to men!

*Henry Wadsworth Longfellow, 1807-1882*
*From CHRISTMAS BELLS*

Somehow, not only for Christmas,
But all the long year through,
The joy that you give to others
Is the joy that comes back to you;
And the more you spend in blessing
The poor and lonely and sad,
The more of your heart's possessing
Returns to make you glad.

*John Greenleaf Whittier, 1807-1892*
*THE JOY OF GIVING*

I have always thought of Christmastime, when it has come round, as a good time; a kind, forgiving, charitable, pleasant time; the only time I know of in the long calendar of the year when men and women seem by one consent to open their shut-up hearts freely, and to think of people below them as if they really were fellow passengers, and not another race of creatures bound on other journeys. And therefore, though it has never put a scrap of gold or silver in my pocket, I believe that it has done me good, and will do me good, and I say, God bless it!

*Charles Dickens, 1812-1870*
*THE CHRISTMAS CAROL*

What can I give him
Poor as I am;
If I were a shepherd,
I would give him a lamb.
If I were a wise man,
I would do my part.
But what can I give him?
I will give him my heart.

*Christina Rossetti, 1830-1894*
*MY GIFT*

# Candlelight

How far the Christmas candle
Throws its beams of yellow light
Across the silent snowdrifts
And through the darkest night.

The warm and friendly beacon
Lights a pathway through the snow,
And quietly shows strangers
The way that they should go.

The brightly glowing candle
Beams a message of good cheer.
Within its golden burning
Shines a welcome far and near.

What a comfort to the stranger!
What a blessed, cheering sight
To gaze upon the beauty
Of a window warm with candlelight!

*Joy Belle Burgess*

In Anticipation of

*Christmas*

# In the Week When Christmastime Comes

This is the week when Christmas comes.

Let every pudding burst with plums,
And every tree bear dolls and drums,
    In the week when Christmas comes.

Let every hall have boughs of green,
With berries glowing in between,
    In the week when Christmas comes.

Let every doorstep have a song
Sounding the dark street along,
    In the week when Christmas comes.

Let every steeple ring a bell
With a joyful tale to tell,
    In the week when Christmas comes.

Let every night put forth a star
To show us where the heavens are,
    In the week when Christmas comes.

Let every stable have a lamb
Sleeping warm beside its dam,
    In the week when Christmas comes.

This is the week when Christmas comes.

*Eleanor Farjeon*

# Santa's Coming

The stars are frosty against the sky,
   and the north wind whistles shrill;
The snow is blowing against the house
   and drifting across the hill.
And away up north a reindeer team
   is harnessed and eager for flight;
The sleigh is loaded with lovely toys,
   for Santa Claus comes tonight!

And now he is ready. The little team
   leaps into the northern sky
Lighter than any wind that blows . . .
   Gracious, how fast they fly!
The gay sweet bells on Santa's sleigh
   play a merry tinkling tune,
And Santa laughs as his little team
   wins a race with the man in the moon.

Faster than ever they're coming now
   down the slippery Milky Way
(They have to return to their home,
   you know, ere the dawn of Christmas Day).
And Santa has many a mile to go
   and many a task to do,
For he must visit boys and girls,
   everyone, including you.

Hush, I think I hear the sleigh bells,
   hear the patter of a hoof,
Hear old Santa's cheery chuckle
   as he walks across our roof.
He'll come sliding down the chimney,
   for he doesn't mind the fire,
And in the pack upon his back
   he'll have your heart's desire.

Oh, eager restless little girl,
   now hurry into bed,
And draw the blankets tight
   and warm above your curly head.
Oh, close your eyes, you funny child . . .
   now don't you hear him creep?
Santa never visits little ones
   who aren't fast asleep!

*Mrs. Roy L. Peifer*

*Photo opposite*
*Ralph D. Luedtke*

# It's Getting to Be Christmas

It's getting to be Christmas.
   There's spruce tang on the breeze.
And parking lots grow sudden woods
   Of pointed, blue-green trees.

And doors and windows come alive
   With crimson bows and gold
On prickly wreaths of evergreens
   Like laughter in the cold.

And cookies baked as trees and stars
   Or boots for Santa's feet
And sugar-sprinkled reindeer teams
   As crisp as they are sweet.

It's getting to be Christmas,
   Your heart begins to twirl
Like stripes around a candy cane,
   A dizzy joyful whirl.

The doorbell rings and packages
   Arrive to disappear.
And fingers ride on lips to guard
   Surprises that are near.

The taste of glue is on your tongue
   And carols fill your head;
The gifts you've wrapped and sealed
   "With Love,"
Safely hid beneath your bed.

It's getting to be Christmas,
The darkness is aglow
With windows framing lighted rooms,
With gleams of falling snow;

With houses wound in rainbow lights . . .
Green, orange, blues and reds . . .
With candles topped by nodding flames
Like elves with fiery heads;

And with wondrous shimmering
Of wishes in the air,
With starlight blue on drifted yards,
With gladness everywhere.

It's getting to be Christmas,
Gay bells hang on the tree.
And every question that you ask
Is answered, "Wait and see."

The shepherds kneel in cotton snow
With wise men in a ring
As once real shepherds knelt in wait
To praise the newborn King.

Your face is washed, your prayers are said,
The hours left are few;
Your bed is warm; there's not a sound . . .
The world is waiting, too.

It's getting to be Christmas,
You'll lie with eyes shut tight.
As often as you open them,
It's still the same long night.

It's getting to be, getting to be . . .
The clock tickticks away.
You lift your head; could you have heard
The jingle of a sleigh?

Then bells within you start to chime,
You bounce up like a ball.
The sky is pale! The day is here!
A Merry Christmas all!

*Beverly Butler*

# Is There a Santa Claus?

By popular demand, we are again featuring this famous editorial which first appeared in *The Sun*, September 21, 1897.

We take pleasure in answering at once and thus prominently the communication below, expressing at the same time our great gratification that its faithful author is numbered among the friends of *The Sun*:

> Dear Editor:
> I am 8 years old.
> Some of my little friends say there is no Santa Claus.
> Papa says, "If you see it in *The Sun*, it's so."
> Please tell me the truth, is there a Santa Claus?
>
> Virginia O'Hanlon,           115 West 95th Street

Virginia, your little friends are wrong. They have been affected by the skepticism of a skeptical age. They do not believe except they see. They think that nothing can be which is not comprehensible by their little minds. All minds, Virginia, whether they be men's or children's, are little. In this great universe of ours, man is a mere insect, an ant, in his intellect, as compared with the boundless world about him, as measured by the intelligence capable of grasping the whole of truth and knowledge.

Yes, Virginia, there is a Santa Claus. He exists as certainly as love and generosity and devotion exist; and you know that they abound and give to your life its highest beauty and joy. Alas! how dreary would be the world if there were no Santa Claus! It would be as dreary as if there were no Virginias. There would be no childlike faith then, no poetry, no romance to make tolerable this existence. We should have no enjoyment, except in sense and sight. The eternal light with which childhood fills the world would be extinguished.

Not believe in Santa Claus! You might as well not believe in fairies! You might get your papa to hire men to watch in all the chimneys on Christmas Eve to catch Santa Claus, but even if they did not see Santa Claus coming down, what would that prove? Nobody sees Santa Claus, but that is no sign that there is no Santa Claus. The most real things in the world are those that neither children nor men can see. Did you ever see fairies dancing on the lawn? Of course not, but that's no proof that they are not there. Nobody can conceive or imagine all the wonders there are unseen and unseeable in the world.

You tear apart the baby's rattle and see what makes the noise inside; but there is a veil covering the unseen world which not the strongest man, nor even the united strength of all the strongest men that ever lived, could tear apart. Only faith, fancy, poetry, love, romance, can push aside that curtain and view and picture the supernal beauty and glory beyond. Is it all real? Ah, Virginia, in all this world there is nothing else real and abiding.

No Santa Claus! Thank God he lives, and he lives forever. A thousand years from now, Virginia, nay, ten times ten thousand years from now, he will continue to make glad the heart of childhood.

*Francis P. Church*

*Painting opposite*
*George Hinke*

Geo. Hinke

# Festive December

WINTER COMES TO STILLMEADOW, sifting down with the sifting snow. The snowfall gives a strange impermanence to the countryside, blurring the far hills, silvering the pond, tipping the mailbox with ermine. The air itself seems silver-white. When I go out to fill the bird feeders, starry flakes melt cool on my cheeks.

The chickadees chatter, nuthatches slide down the tree trunks, blue jays cry angrily from the sugar maples. Juncos are almost under my feet. The relationship of birds and man is a rewarding one, for even the shiest birds respond to friendship. The bridge between me and mine is an easy one, composed of sunflower seeds, chick feed, raisins, bread crumbs, suet cakes. As I talk to the gathering wings, I am answered by the dipping toward my hands. I cannot help thinking that barriers between people—of all nationalities—should not be insurmountable, for human beings are of one species. Perhaps the secret is in personal giving. What is held out in the open hand means more than allotments.

The valley begins to look festive as December goes along. The giant pine at the village center glows with light. Christmas wreaths blossom on every door. George Tomey decorates the market, and Green's store looks like a Christmas party. The post office is piled so high with packages that I can barely see the heads of the postal workers.

As Christmas approaches, Erma helps me decorate Stillmeadow. Mistletoe, holly, and pine branches give a festive look to the old house. Gay greeting cards decorate two of the mantels, the corner cupboard where I keep the milk glass, and the bookshelves. Christmas candles go on the wide window ledges but never on the tree, for I am afraid they might start a fire. Bowls of fruit are temporary decorations, for the children start to eat the fruit as soon as they arrive for the holidays, and the bowl on the coffee bench has to be refilled several times a day.

The tree goes in the front living room, and we put our packages under it. Christmas Eve is my special time. When the children were growing up, Jill used to pop corn and set out the wooden dough trough, filled with nuts and polished apples, while I

read Dickens's *A Christmas Carol* aloud. I know it by heart because it was read to me every Christmas when I was growing up. It was a link between the generations. Nowadays, however, the very young do not make for quiet reading. Even after they are tucked away, they want a drink of water, or they lose their go-to-sleep rabbit over the crib wall, or *something.*

But after they finally go to sleep, the adults sit around the fire and sing carols and talk. I have a chance to look at the three grown-up children—my daughter, and Jill's son and daughter—and they are beautiful to me. Their young thoughtful faces have not really changed.

How far they have traveled since *they* were asking for a drink of water at bedtime! And how proud I am of them. Sometimes when I go out to the back kitchen to let Holly in, I imagine the drying bunny suits and mittens and hoods belong to my three. Time is a curious thing. Those bunny suits belong to Muffin, Anne, Jamie, and Betsy, and the larger snow outfits to the two older grandchildren (who also have ice skates, for fun on the pond).

This is an uneasy world, but at this holy time, I find faith anew in the power of love and goodwill. My belief in goodness is not shaken. The babe born in a manger brought an enduring message to mankind. He was indeed to become the Prince of Peace, and is so still.

The snow stops falling, and the lovely light of a distant untroubled moon makes magic in swamp and meadow. The house settles into quiet. I go out with the cockers and Irish for a last look at night. On Christmas Eve, my Honey—the golden cocker who companioned me for fourteen years—moves beside me. Jill stands in the lighted doorway. Remembrance is a form of meeting, says Gibran, and so it is.

Inevitably, as I turn out the lights and the embers die into ash, Connie comes softly down the stairs. "I just wanted to say what a lovely Christmas Eve, Mamma," she says. And this, of course, is my best present of all.

I think of neighbors I have never seen and pray for peace and goodwill for us all.

*Gladys Taber*

*In Anticipation of Christmas* **57**

# The Wonder of Christmas

The wonder of Christmas is soft candlelight;
The wonder of Christmas, a song in the night.
Hearth fires glowing and snow on the trees,
The wonder of Christmas is all of these.

A fairy-like touch of holly and pine;
A package that's wrapped with tinsel and twine;
Light-hearted children laughing in glee . . .
The wonder of Christmas is beauty to see.

There are scents from the kitchen of goodies
   to eat,
And the last minute shoppers are trudging
   the street.
But far in the distance the bells sound clear . . .
The wonder of Christmas is everywhere.

The wonder is felt as a friend meets a friend
With that age-old greeting of "Goodwill to men."
The rapture expressed on one special day
When the worshiper kneels in silence to pray.

*Estelle Ellington Platt*

*Painting opposite*
*Frances Hook*

# There's Christmas in the Air

December brings the best of all . . .
The birthday of the Christ Child dear,
The openhearted Christmas Day,
The best loved day of all the year.

This time of year we feel closer
To nations, all the world around;
With open hearts we greet mankind,
And tolerance and love abound.

Our friendly town is all astir
With busy shoppers rushing round;
To buy for each one on their list
Means shopping all around the town.

The spirit of Christmas abides
As strangers smile at all they meet;
They nod and pass the time of day,
And happily, old friends they greet.

The magic hours of Christmastime
When families together walk and play;
The gifts to wrap, the tree to trim,
And secrets quickly put away.

The odors from the kitchen come
Of spicy cookies, hot fruitcake;
The buttery smell of fresh popcorn,
And candy bubbling in the make.

The children share in everything
As in and out they race like wild;
But Christmas is unthinkable
Without at least one little child.

The twinkling trees from windows gleam
And carols linger in the air;
The stores are like a fairyland
And Christmas spirit's everywhere.

*Gertrude Bryson Holman*

# Christmas Dreaming

The small child lies asleep at last,
A favorite toy clutched in his grasp.
One could not know or e'er conceive
What dreams are his on Christmas Eve.

Perhaps he floats among the stars
And smiles at Venus, winks at Mars,
Or rides a cloud to Neverland
To walk with fairies hand-in-hand.

Perchance he sails the bounding main
Where scores of pirates gained their fame
And finds a carefully hidden lair
With secret treasure buried there.

What-e'er his dreams this Christmas Eve,
They're sure to fade, then take their leave
When Christmas Day dawns bright and clear
Mid shouts of "Santa has been here!"

*Ned Nichols*

*Photo opposite*
*Michael Saunders*

# The Visitations of
# *Christmas*

# Home for Christmas

Away from the busy sights and sounds
I take the road toward home,
Back to the hills and the valleys,
Back where I loved to roam.

The snow is white and glistening,
The stars shine bright above;
I'm going home for Christmas,
Home to those I love.

The folks will be there waiting
With a smile and open arms;
I'll find warmth and laughter there,
The wealth of homey charms.

There'll be a Christmas tree in the window
As friends and neighbors gather round
To sing the songs of Christmas;
And joy shall there abound.

The road seems long and winding
But there's happiness at the end;
For I'm going home for Christmas,
And home is round the bend.

*Gladys Billings Bratton*

# Christmas Cards

This time of year, I always stand
Beside the door to wait
Until I hear the postman lift
The latch upon the gate.
I run to meet him, for I know
He will most certainly
Reach down into his sack to find
Some Christmas cards for me.

In many shapes and sizes,
They come from far and near,
And each of them recalls a face
And friendship very dear.
Some come in bright red envelopes
With holly berry seals,
And others may arrive in white
With scenes of winter fields.

And then there are the special ones,
With edges trimmed in gold,
Much too thick, and long, and wide
For my mailbox to hold.
I watch the stack grow larger,
With humble joy, to see
The many folks throughout the year
Who have remembered me.

And sitting at my rosewood desk
Till long into the night,
I choose my own cards carefully;
And then I start to write.
My heart is filled with memories,
Bright as a candle flame,
And I address the envelopes,
But love's hand signs my name.

*Grace E. Easley*

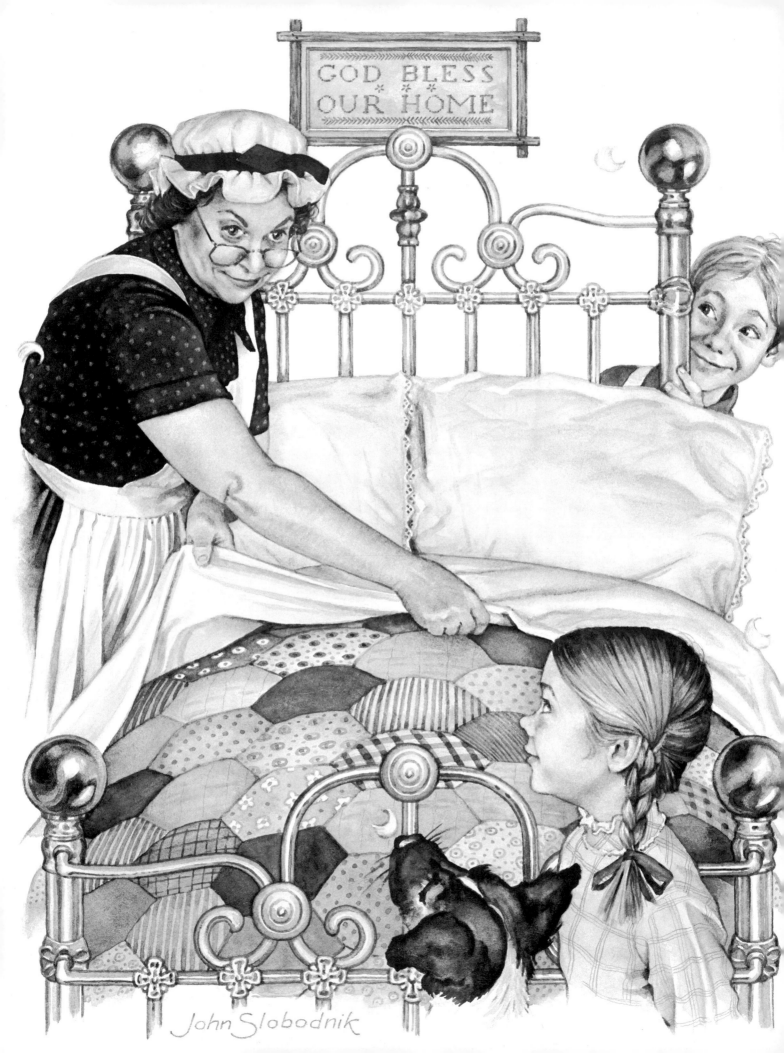

# The Old-Fashioned Featherbed

Sleeping at Grandma's house was like sleeping on a thick, fluffy cloud, a pleasant experience to be anticipated and enjoyed. Climbing into that cozy bank of down in an unheated room, sinking into the arms of Morpheus in the warm featherbed, was an unexcelled luxury. Sleep came quickly and morning much too soon.

No one was allowed to make Grandma's beds. It was a privilege she reserved for herself, and we were satisfied when we were permitted to assist. No one could make the beds like Grandma, and she was very fussy about how it was done. They were never made until all the bedclothes had been removed and the bed thoroughly aired, so it was not until the breakfast had been cleared away, the floors swept, and the rest of the house dusted and tidied that she directed her attention to the bedrooms.

It was a marvelous experience to watch Grandma at the task of bedmaking. To her, it was not just a routine chore, but an artistic achievement. First the featherbed was shaken, then it was turned over and shaken again until it was as light and fluffy as the meringue on one of her excellent lemon pies. With a deft hand she pounded, punched, patted, and smoothed. Through the heavy ticking she wheedled and coaxed the elusive feathers until every one was in exactly the right place. Only when it was as smooth as a mountain lake on a calm summer day was Grandma satisfied. Very carefully the sheets and patchwork quilts were spread over the puffy mound, and the pillows piled against the head of the huge brass bed and tucked into a neat roll. The snowy white spread left the bed looking like a giant, frosty cream puff.

The unpardonable sin was to sit on the bed or in some way dent that flawless surface. When Grandma had finished, we looked with admiration at her masterpiece and wished we could bounce in its billowy depths.

Grandma has been gone these many years, and the featherbed has long since disappeared. The feathers were stuffed into several pillows that have never lost their buoyancy.

When winter temperatures drop to zero and below, and the chill creeps into my bed, I remember those luxurious nights and wish I could sleep once more in Grandma's featherbed.

*June C. Garfield*

*Painting overleaf*
*George Hinke*

# They'll Be Home for Christmas

Jingle bells and tinsel
And trimmings tucked away
Are coming from their wrappings
To grace the holiday.

Cookies in the making,
And presents ten feet tall . . .
Songs to sing and bells to ring
And Christmas cheer for all.

Dreams and hopes and wishes
Will all be coming true.
But best of all,
The ones you love
Are coming home to you!

*Nelle Hardgrove*

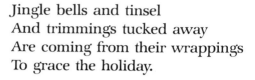

# Going Home

"We're going home for Christmas,"
Oh, how I love the phrase.
It brings to mind fond memories
Of bygone holidays.

I see again a Christmas tree
Bedecked with tinsel and lights,
And hear familiar voices
Echoing through the night.

Church bells ring in the distance,
A choir sings its praise,
And we remember how it was
In those joyous yesterdays.

"We're going home for Christmas,"
A phrase forever sweet . . .
A time for sharing memories
As loved ones once again meet.

*Shirley Sallay*

# The Trimming of the Tree

What gayer experience can there be
Than the trimming of a Christmas tree?
With gentle touch and sparkling eyes,
We take up every new surprise
As though it were some jewel rare,
Deserving of our most tender care.

With fragile brightly colored things
Like tinseled bells and beads on strings,
We feel our ecstasy increase
As we create a masterpiece
Of startling beauty, fraught with glee,
From what was just a plain green tree.

Then when each bauble has been hung
And when the final rope is strung,
Its lighted loveliness imparts
A glow of warmth to all our hearts.
Much less would Yuletide pleasures be
Without the trimming of the tree.

*Nadine Brothers Lybarger*

# Christmas Eve
# Tree Trimming Party

## Hot Apricot Grog

Makes 7½ cups

  1 46-ounce can apricot nectar
  2 tablespoons lemon juice
1½ cups brandy
   Lemon slices
   Whole cloves

Pour apricot nectar, lemon juice, and brandy into a large saucepan. Bring to a simmer. Ladle into mugs or punch cups. Garnish each serving with a lemon slice studded with a clove.

## Cranberry Punch

Makes 30 servings

  4 cups cranberry juice
1½ cups sugar
  4 cups pineapple juice
  1 tablespoon almond extract
  2 quarts ginger ale

Combine first 4 ingredients. Stir until sugar is dissolved; chill. Add ginger ale just before serving.

## Christmas Cider

Makes 16 servings

  2 quarts apple cider
  1 cup brown sugar
  3 3-inch sticks cinnamon
  1 teaspoon whole cloves
  1 teaspoon salt

Heat cider to boiling. Lower heat; add remaining ingredients. Simmer 15 minutes. Strain and serve.

## Holiday Wassail

Makes 4 cups

1½ cups sugar
  4 cups boiling water
  3 whole allspice
  6 whole cloves
  1 tablespoon ground ginger
  1 1-inch stick cinnamon
1⅓ cups orange juice
 ⅔ cup lemon juice

Combine sugar and 2 cups of the boiling water; boil 5 minutes. Add spices; cover and let stand 1 hour. Add remaining water and fruit juices; mix well. Strain. Heat to boiling. Serve immediately.

*Cranberry Punch, above*

# O to Be in Iowa

O to be in Iowa, now that Christmas is here! We had a lovely snowfall on the nineteenth, and the sound of sleigh bells fills the air. Racy cutters, with their smartly curved dashboards in highly polished red or green, vie for position with the big bobsleds from the lumberyard. Everywhere in the crisp pure air sounds the music of the big Swedish sleigh bells, the open shaft bells, the gong shaft bells, the pole and saddle chimes, and the entrancing silvery Russian saddle chimes. Everybody has got their genuine buffalo or shiny plush robes out of mothballs. Meanwhile the automobiles go puffing about blowing steam most amazingly and clanking their tire chains in the snowy streets.

It is very cold and the train whistles have a different frosty freezing tone. Walking down the street your shoes make squeaky noises on the packed snow. Jack Frost has worked his artistry on windowpanes. Noses are rather red and all the feminine band are carrying their muffs. Small boys and girls are wound around and around with scarves so that only their peeping eyes can be seen between scarf and knitted cap.

The stores look very pretty this year. Papa's EMPORIUM is trimmed with tinsel garlands, imitation holly vines, and large red tissue paper bells. Potterveld's drugstore has two large palmetto palms in the windows and artificial poinsettias. The palms are dried in a special way and keep forever. Harriet's papa's "Oriental Sweet Shoppe" has pennants spelling "Merry Christmas" and red festooning.

It is fun to go into the EMPORIUM and see everybody carefully picking out gifts for their loved ones. (Also for the ones they *don't* love but have to give presents to!) I tell you, the cash trolleys are really whizzing. Business is so brisk that Papa is waiting on trade right alongside Walter, Fanny, Emily, Mrs. Kowalski, and all the other clerks.

Of course, there was entertainment at school on the last day. I was one of the "wise men," as usual. I do believe that if I ran away from home to New York and became an actress,

I would end up on Broadway as a "wise man."

I assisted at the party for the children in the Second Presbyterian Church vestry, but for the first time Santa had not left a gift for me. "You're a young lady now, Julia," said horrid, old, skinny Mrs. Coots. I confess I went into the cloak room to hide my tears. I was too proud after that to take the customary, gay little box of hard candy. I gave mine to little Lucy Dubois.

O well, "Say la vee," as Papa says, which is French and means "That's life for you."

*Richard Bissell*

# Skaters at Dusk

At the bend of the river the skaters glide
Like swift-winged swallows upon their way.
There, where the ice is smooth and wide,
They circle and wing, they lean and sway.

The wind dies down with the coming night;
The purple and crimson afterglow
Is darkly etched with the eager flight
Where the swaying, swinging skaters go.

Their laughter echoes, their voices ring,
Forward and backward they swoop and wheel—
Sharp on the air the zip and zing
Where the ice is cut by the flying steel.

Low in the west, a star's clear flame;
The red-lit river grows dark at last.
A boy's voice calls another's name—
Already the supper hour is past.

The clank of unloosed skates, the tread
Of tingling feet on the frozen ground,
And hungry as wolves, and ready for bed,
The tired skaters are homeward bound.

*Grace Noll Crowell*

*Painting opposite*
*Maud-Misha Petersham*

# The Celebration of
## *Christmas*

# Sleigh Ride

We're off and away o'er the beautiful snow
On the wings of our Christmas sleigh,
Splitting the air with the echoing swells
Of laughter and song today.

We ride in the wake of our lively steeds
That race through the wintry chill,
That canter and gallop with marvelous ease
Over the meadow and hill.

And, oh, hear the tinkle they shake from the bells,
The music of mirth from our sleigh;
The notes that come floating gentle and clear
To mark our melodious way.

A ripple of laughter is rousing the hill
As we glide across the snow,
While happiness shines from our radiant eyes
In the warmth of friendship's glow.

Still on and away o'er the glittering track
On the wings of our magic sleigh,
We ride into the whirl of fluttering flakes
And the joy of Christmas Day!

*Joy Belle Burgess*

# It's a Great Night

It's a great night for gathering round the fire
And spinning a yarn or two;
It's grand to be cozily snuggled up in
A favorite armchair, too.

It's snowing without and the winds do howl—
How comfortable by the fire!
See how the shadows are cast on the walls
As the flames lick up still higher.

In due time we'll roast chestnuts by the fire—
What choice morsels they'll make!
We might run through photograph albums then,
Just for the old-time's sake!

We'll talk of our friends and our blessings, too,
And the beauties of true goodwill;
It's a great night for gathering round the fire
While the winds outside grow chill.

*Georgia B. Adams*

# Christmas Windows

There are dreams in Christmas windows,
Dreams in every pane.
Some see gaiety and laughter
Or perhaps a wintry plain

Where one night a star
Shed a brilliant light,
And startled sleepy shepherds
Watching o'er their flocks that night.

Some see dim reflections
Of Christmas long ago.
Others see some carolers
Tramping through the snow.

Others may see worshipers
With heads bowed in prayer;
Some may reflect longingly
On loved ones who are not there.

Or maybe there are visions
Of a train or a doll that walks,
Or a pretty picture book,
Or some brightly painted blocks.

Yes, dreams are in Christmas windows,
And the message they impart
Is really the feeling of Christmas
We hold in our own heart.

*Shirley McCalla Cowart*

# Christmas Chant

Candle, candle
  burning bright
On our window-
  sill tonight,
Like the shining
  Christmas star
Guiding shepherds
  from afar,
Lead some weary
  traveler here,
That he may share
  our Christmas cheer.

*Isabel Shaw*

*The Celebration of Christmas* **85**

# Our Gifts to Our Children

First and Foremost
*We give them the most precious of all gifts: the principles of
brotherly love and the love of God, as taught so many years ago
by Christ, whose birth we celebrate.*

We Give Them Our Attention
*For one day it will be too late.*

We Give Them a Sense of Value
*A place for the individual in the scheme of things, with all
that accrues to the individual: self-reliance, courage,
conviction, self-respect and the respect of others.*

We Give Them a Sense of Humor
*Laughter leavens life.*

We Give Them the Meaning of Discipline
*If we falter at discipline, life will do it for us.*

We Give Them the Will to Work
*Satisfying work is not the lasting joy, but knowing that a
job is well done, is.*

We Give Them the Talent for Sharing
*That it's not so much that we give, as to what we share.*

We Give Them the Love of Justice
*The bulwark against violence and oppression, and the
repository of human dignity.*

We Give Them the Passion of Truth
*Founded on precept of example, truth is the beginning of every
good thing; the power and the faith engendering mutual trust.*

We Give Them the Beacon of Hope
*Which lights all darkness.*

We Give Them Knowledge of Being Loved
*Beyond the demand for reciprocity, praise or blame, for those
loved are never lost.*

What Shall We Give the Children?
*The open sky, the brown earth, the leafy trees, the golden sand,
the blue water, the stars in their courses, and the awareness of
these; birdsongs, butterflies, clouds and rainbows, sunlight,
moonlight, firelight; a large hand reaching down for a small hand,
impromptu praise, an unexpected kiss, a straight answer, the
glisten of enthusiasm and the sense of wonder, long days to be
merry in and nights without fear, and the memory of a good home.*

These Things We Shall Give the Children

*Author Unknown*          *The Celebration of Christmas*  **87**

# Winter Fun

Over the hills we go coasting down,
Then across the lake like a mirror round;
On the smooth white slope we start from above,
Then down we go as swift as a dove.

Out in the yard right by our gate,
The big, white snowman we like to make.
We shape it with snow, white and clean;
With fir moss for a beard,
It's just the thing.
A carrot for a nose and apples for eyes,
It makes him look so very wise.

Down on the pond there is everyone
Skating together—oh, what fun!
A figure eight, a tug of war,
There's a bonfire blazing on the shore.

We'll warm our hands before we run;
There's hot chocolate waiting for everyone.
We'll sing together for good cheer;
It's the merriest, happiest time of the year.

*Irene Lloyd Goodwin*

# Skating Pond

They dart about like water bugs
  With waving arms and sprawling legs,
Some as graceful as the swans
  While others stiff as wooden pegs.
And yet, the fun they have is worth
  More than the minted gold of earth.

The ice is clear as painted glass,
  Bordered by heaps of drifted snow;
The winter sky above the trees
  Almost as blue as indigo;
A setting lovely as a gem
  Set in a vacant lot for them.

They swoop, and dip, and whirl, and dart,
  Fall with a thud and slide a bit;
Crawl on all fours like tiny bears,
  Yet never seem to tire of it;
But up and at it once again,
  Crusted with snow like frozen men.

Their little cheeks are warm and red
  Like apples on the rosy side;
Snowsuits of red, and green, and blue—
  The little bodies tucked inside
Are warm as kittens wrapped in wool—
  Lovely to look at . . . beautiful.

Here on this vacant lot is heard
  Young laughter merry as a lark,
The gay voice of a little girl,
  A tiny dog's excited bark,
Where all the bells of heaven chime
Under the spell of wintertime.

*Edna Jaques*

89

# A Christmas Pup

Oh, what an absolute delight!
   Just see what happened Christmas night.
A tiny pup—cute, wiggly, smart—
   Came right into my eager heart.

I said "hello" and picked him up;
   He was such a naughty pup.
He yawned and tried to get away
   Because he thought he'd rather play.

So much to see, so many lights,
   A dozen other tempting sights;
He had to wrestle with the rug
   Before he paused to give a hug.

He gave each ornament a sniff,
   Then tore the bows from every gift.
Worn out at last, he came my way
   And love came in my heart to stay.

*Alice Leedy Mason*

*Photo opposite*
*Clifford Carroll*

"AN OBJECT OF ENVY."

# Christmas Sled

Oh, for the winters that used to be!
The winters that only a boy may see!
Rich with the snowflakes' rush and swirl,
Keen as a diamond, pure as a pearl,
Brimming with healthful, rollicking fun,
Sweet with their rest when the play was done,
With kindly revels each day decreed,
And a Christmas sled for the royal steed.

Down from the crest with shrill hurray!
Clear the track, there! Out of the way!
Scarcely touching the path beneath,
Scarce admitting of breath to breathe,
Dashing along, with leap and swerve,
Over the crossing, round the curve.
Talk of your flying machines! Instead,
Give me the swoop of that Christmas sled.

*Author Unknown*

# A Christmas Kitten

Our Christmas kitten's really bright;
   She's standing guard this Christmas night.
Sometimes she jumps from stair to stair,
   Or hides beneath the rocking chair.

She's keeping watch from dusk till dawn;
   Something moves and the chase is on!
Papers rustle in a box;
   A search is made of Christmas socks.

A toy mouse, a catnip ball,
   Some scraps of yarn out in the hall,
The Christmas crèche, a cookie plate,
   All these she must investigate.

But not just now—it's time for bed;
   A place to lay her weary head.
Content this is the place for her,
   She drops her guard and starts to purr!

*Alice Leedy Mason*

*Photo opposite*
*Clifford Carroll*

The Inspiration of

*Christmas*

# One Small Child

One little child . . . no more, no less—
And could his mother Mary guess
Salvation for the human race
Depended on that night, that place?
And did she know this child would cause
All heaven to rock with glad applause?
Would cause the angels to rehearse
Their midnight song of sacred verse?
Would cause a star of strange design
To leave its orbit, and to shine
A brilliant path, from east to west?
Would cause wise men to choose the best
Of hoarded treasure, and to search
The nations from a camel perch?
Would make a king (in craven fear)
Destroy small man-children near?
To this small child the nation thrilled,
For he was prophecy fulfilled.
But could his mother even guess,
While rocking him with tenderness,
The whole import of his advent . . .
This one small child, from heaven sent.

*Esther S. Buckwalter*

# A Time for Giving

What are you giving for Christmas? God the Father scattered the Milky Way across the skies and thought about Christmas. God the Son thought often of the day that God would speak the Word, and he, "Christ," would be born. He would gaze with "baby eyes" upon the very creatures he had made. God the Holy Spirit, moving as a shadow upon the face of the waters in Genesis days, knew one day it would be necessary to move again. This time he would overshadow Mary's womb, that the child born of her should be called the "Son of God."

As Elisabeth was thinking about the promised gifts of God's special people, God was busy wrapping up his Christmas present in heaven in humanity's wrapping paper. Christmas came early, just for Elisabeth. She had room in her inn for Mary, the outcast, ostracized, pregnant girl. God pulled the wrapping paper back just a little to let her have a peek at his present, and Elisabeth's baby leaped in her womb for joy, and she was filled with the Holy Ghost. And so she spake with a loud voice, "Blessed art thou among women, and blessed is the fruit of thy womb. And whence is this to me that the mother of my Lord should come to me. For, lo, as soon as the voice of thy salutation sounded in mine ears, the babe leaped in my womb for joy. And blessed are you for believing, Mary, for there shall be a performance of those things which were told you from the Lord" (Luke 1:42-45).

Encouraged and strengthened by her cousin, Mary, too, prepared. She believed the Anointed One must come, and soon, and by her holy character made ready to acknowledge her Messiah and yield him her allegiance. Because of her humility, she never in her wildest dreams imagined that she would actually become personally involved. But God couldn't have a Christmas without a Mary. He needed a body to live in!

Mary bowed her head. She bowed her will; she gave her body. She whispered, "Behold the handmaid of the Lord. Be it unto me according to thy Word."

What about Joseph? What did he give? Mary had told him about Christ, and the shock, the hurt, and the jealousy just completely engulfed him. How could he account for the confusing change in her character? How could she blame God for her sin? Tossing in torment upon his bed, Joseph decided to reject Mary and the baby. But God knew his Joseph, his godliness, his honesty, his love for God and for Mary. God knew Joseph was a man who had only to be convinced of the truth by divine revelation; and then on the strength of a dream, he'd rise and give Christ his reputation and his care for the rest of his life.

"But while he thought of these things, the angel of the Lord appeared to him in a dream saying, 'Joseph, thou son of David, don't be frightened to take unto thee Mary, thy wife. For that which is conceived in her is of the Holy Ghost. And she shall bring forth a son and you shall call him Jesus, for he shall save his people from their sins'" (Matthew 1:20, 21).

The party had begun! Herod was invited. "Bring your gifts," invited the wise men.

And he came, but with his gift wrapped in hate and tied in murder. He came screaming, "I will not have this man to reign over me. I'll be my own ruler, in my own kingdom, and run my own life." And he gave his gift, the gift of rejection.

The shepherds gave their time. They ran in haste to find out if all that heaven said about this earthly babe was true. Surely this was worth the gift of time. Time to leave their flocks, their daily work. Time to kneel before their infant Maker, to smell the smells in the dark cave, and realize he didn't care, he only loved so much he had to be born then.

And the innkeeper? He did what he could. Mary and Joseph knocked on the door of his life, on behalf of Jesus Christ, and they asked him to make room. And he did. He received Christ and he gave Christ a gift, his stable.

Christmas is for giving. God gave his son; Elisabeth, her praise; Mary, her body; Joseph, his reputation; Herod, his rejection; the shepherds, their time; and the innkeeper, his stable. Tell me, do you see your present there?

*Jill Briscoe*

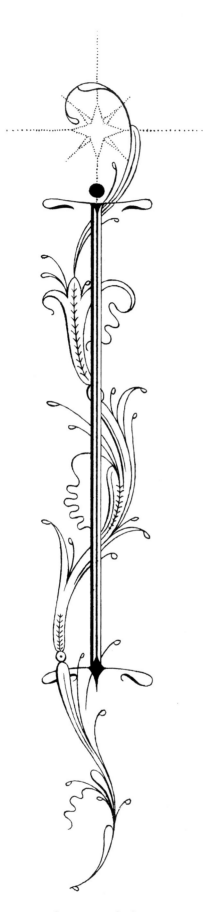

*"For unto us a child is born, unto us a son is given: and the government shall be upon his shoulder: and his name shall be called*

# The Gospel According to Luke and Matthew

nd it came to pass in those days, that there went out a decree from Caesar Augustus, that all the world should be taxed. And all went to be taxed, every one into his own city. And Joseph also went up from Galilee, out of the city of Nazareth, into Judaea, unto the city of David, which is called Bethlehem; (because he was of the house and lineage of David:) To be taxed with Mary his espoused wife, being great with child. And so it was, that, while they were there, the days were accomplished that she should be delivered. And she brought forth her first born son, and wrapped him in swaddling clothes, and laid him in a manger; because there was no room for them in the inn.

And there were in the same country shepherds abiding in the field, keeping watch over their flock by night. And, lo, the angel of the Lord came upon them, and the glory of the Lord shone round about them: and they were sore afraid. And the angel said unto them, Fear not: for, behold, I bring you good tidings of great joy, which shall be to all people. For unto you is born this day in the city of David a Saviour, which is Christ the Lord. And this shall be a sign unto you; Ye shall find the babe wrapped in swaddling clothes, lying in a manger. And suddenly there was with the angel a multitude of the heavenly host praising God, and saying, Glory to God in the highest, and on earth peace, good will toward men.

And it came to pass, as the angels were gone away from them into heaven, the shepherds said one to another, Let us now go even unto Bethlehem, and see this thing which is come to pass, which the Lord hath made known unto us. And they came with haste, and found Mary, and Joseph, and the babe lying in a manger. And when they had seen it, they made known abroad the saying which was told them concerning this child. And all they that heard it wondered at those things which were told them by the shepherds (Luke 2:1-18).

*Wonderful, Counsellor, The mighty God, The everlasting Father, The Prince of Peace"*
*(Isaiah 9:6)*

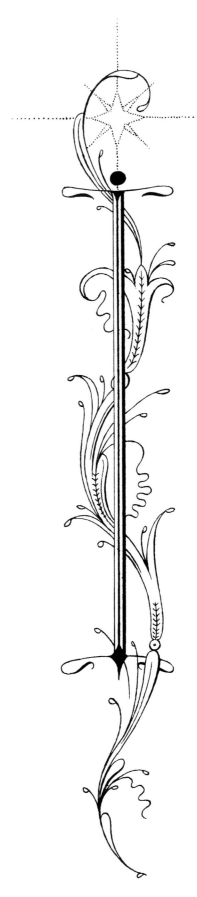

ow when Jesus was born in Bethlehem of Judaea in the days of Herod the king, behold, there came wise men from the east to Jerusalem, saying, Where is he that is born King of the Jews? for we have seen his star in the east, and are come to worship him. When Herod the king had heard these things, he was troubled, and all Jerusalem with him. And when he had gathered all the chief priests and scribes of the people together, he demanded of them where Christ should be born. And they said unto him, In Bethlehem of Judaea: for thus it is written by the prophet, And thou Bethlehem, in the land of Juda, art not the least among the princes of Juda: for out of thee shall come a Governor, that shall rule my people Israel.

Then Herod, when he had privily called the wise men, inquired of them diligently what time the star appeared. And he sent them to Bethlehem, and said, Go and search diligently for the young child; and when ye have found him, bring me word again, that I may come and worship him also. When they had heard the king, they departed; and, lo, the star, which they saw in the east, went before them, till it came and stood over where the young child was. When they saw the star, they rejoiced with exceeding great joy.

And when they were come into the house, they saw the young child with Mary his mother, and fell down and worshipped him: and when they had opened their treasures, they presented unto him gifts; gold, and frankincense and myrrh. And being warned of God in a dream that they should not return to Herod, they departed into their own country another way. And when they were departed, behold, the angel of the Lord appeareth to Joseph in a dream, saying, Arise, and take the young child and his mother, and flee into Egypt, and be thou there until I bring thee word: for Herod will seek the young child to destroy him. When he arose, he took the young child and his mother by night, and departed into Egypt: And was there until the death of Herod: that it might be fulfilled which was spoken of the Lord by the prophet, saying, Out of Egypt have I called my son (Matthew 2:1-15).

*And she brought forth her firstborn son, and wrapped him in swaddling clothes, and laid him in a manger; because there was no room for them in the inn.*

*And they came with haste, and found Mary, and Joseph, and the babe lying in a manger.*

*Luke 2:7, 16*

# It Was Not Strange

He came to be the light,
And so it was not strange
A blazing star should pencil
    out his path
As heaven unfurled its glory
On the night!

Wise kings came from afar!
Could aught more fitting be
Than kneeling sovereigns to greet
The Kings of Kings, sweet baby
Of their star?

With staffs, and sandal-shod,
The shepherds came to search.
Such gentle men . . . it was not
    strange that they
Should find in Bethlehem
The Lamb of God!

*Esther Lloyd Hagg*

*Painting opposite*
*ADORATION OF THE SHEPHERDS*
*A. Van Dyck*
*Kunsthalle, Hamburg, Germany*

# The Ballad of Befana

Befana the Housewife, scrubbing her pane,
Saw three old sages ride down the lane,
Saw three gray travelers pass her door—
Gaspar, Balthazar, Melchior.

"Where journey you, sirs?" she asked of them.
Balthazar answered, "To Bethlehem,

"For we have news of a marvelous thing,
Born in a stable is Christ the King."

"Give him my welcome!"
Then Gaspar smiled,
"Come with us, mistress, to greet the child."

"Oh, happily, happily would I fare,
Were my dusting through and I'd polished the stair."

Old Melchior leaned on his saddle horn,
"Then send but a gift to the small newborn."

"Oh, gladly, gladly I'd send him one,
Were the hearthstone swept and my weaving done.

"As soon as ever I've baked my bread,
I'll fetch him a pillow for his head,
And a coverlet too," Befana said.

"When the rooms are aired and the linen dry,
I'll look at the babe."
But the three rode by.

She worked for a day and a night and a day,
Then, gifts in her hands, took up her way.
But she never could find where the Christ Child lay.

And still she wanders at Christmastide,
Houseless, whose house was all her pride,

Whose heart was tardy, whose gifts were late;
Wanders, and knocks at every gate,
Crying, "Good people, the bells begin!
Put off your toiling and let love in."

*Phyllis McGinley*

*And when they were departed, behold, the angel of the Lord, appeareth to Joseph in a dream, saying, Arise, and take the young child and his mother, and flee into Egypt, and be thou there until I bring thee word: for Herod will seek the young child to destroy Him. When he arose, he took the young child and his mother by night, and departed into Egypt . . .*

*Matthew 2:13-14*

# Flight into Egypt

Out of the land of Judaea
Where wise men had followed the star,
Out of a birthplace so humble
They fled to find safety afar.
Into the night, mysterious,
They hurried past desert and stream
To dwell for a time with strangers,
For they had been warned in a dream.
Simple their trust, unquestioned,
That the child who was placed in their care
Was destined to become the Savior
Of men of goodwill everywhere.
Out of the past spoke the prophet
From writings both sacred and old.
The one who had promised a Savior,
This flight into Egypt foretold.

*Alice Leedy Mason*

*Painting opposite
FLIGHT INTO EGYPT
Bartolome Murillo
(Photo, Three Lions, Inc.)*

# My Christmas Miracle

For many of us, one Christmas stands out from all the others, the one when the meaning of the day shone clearest.

Although I did not guess it, my own "truest" Christmas began on a rainy spring day in the bleakest year of my life. Recently divorced, I was in my 20's, had no job, and was on my way downtown to go the rounds of the employment offices. I had no umbrella, for my old one had fallen apart, and I could not afford another one. I sat down in the streetcar, and there against the seat was a beautiful silk umbrella with a silver handle inlaid with gold and flecks of bright enamel. I had never seen anything so lovely.

I examined the handle and saw a name engraved among the golden scrolls. The usual procedure would have been to turn in the umbrella to the conductor, but on impulse I decided to take it with me and find the owner myself. I got off the streetcar in a downpour and thankfully opened the umbrella to protect myself. Then I searched a telephone book for the name on the umbrella and found it. I called and a lady answered.

Yes, she said in surprise, that was her umbrella, which her parents, now dead, had given her for a birthday present. But, she added, it had been stolen from her locker at school (she was a teacher) more than a year before. She was so excited that I forgot I was looking for a job and went directly to her small house. She took the umbrella, and her eyes filled with tears.

The teacher wanted to give me a reward, but—though twenty dollars was all I had in the world—her happiness at retrieving this special possession was such that to have accepted money would have spoiled something. We talked for a while, and I must have given her my address. I don't remember.

The next six months were wretched. I was able to obtain only temporary employment here and there, for a small salary, though this was what they now call the Roaring Twenties. But I put aside twenty-five or fifty cents when I could afford it for my little girl's Christmas presents. (It took me six months to save eight dollars.) My last job ended the day before Christmas, my thirty dollar rent was soon due, and I had fifteen dollars to my name—which

Peggy and I would need for food. She was home from her convent boarding school and was excitedly looking forward to her gifts the next day, which I had already purchased. I had bought her a small tree, and we were going to decorate it that night.

The stormy air was full of the sound of Christmas merriment as I walked from the streetcar to my small apartment. Bells rang and children shouted in the bitter dusk of the evening, and windows were lighted and everyone was running and laughing. But there would be no Christmas for me, I knew, no gifts, no remembrance whatsoever. As I struggled through the snowdrifts, I just about reached the lowest point in my life. Unless a miracle happened, I would be homeless in January, foodless, jobless. I had prayed steadily for weeks, and there had been no answer but this coldness and darkness, this harsh air, this abandonment. God and men had completely forgotten me. I felt old as death, and as lonely. What was to become of us?

I looked in my mailbox. There were only bills in it, a sheaf of them, and two white envelopes which I was sure contained more bills. I went up three dusty flights of stairs, and I cried, shivering in my thin coat. But I made myself smile so I could greet my little daughter with a pretense of happiness. She opened the door for me and threw herself in my arms, screaming joyously and demanding that we decorate the tree immediately.

Peggy was not yet six years old, and had been alone all day while I worked. She had proudly set our kitchen table for our evening meal and put pans out and the three cans of food which would be our dinner. For some reason, when I looked at those pans and cans, I felt brokenhearted. We would have only hamburgers for our Christmas dinner tomorrow, and gelatin. I stood in the cold little kitchen, and misery overwhelmed me. For the first time in my life, I doubted the existence of God and his mercy, and the coldness in my heart was colder than ice.

The doorbell rang and Peggy ran fleetly to answer it, calling that it must be Santa Claus. Then I heard a man talking heartily to her and went to the door. He was a delivery man, and his arms were full of parcels, and he was laughing at my child's frenzied joy and her dancing. "This is a mistake," I said, but he read the name on the parcels and they were for me. When he had gone I could only stare at the boxes. Peggy and I sat on the floor and opened them. A huge doll, three times the size of the one I had bought for her. Gloves. Candy. A beautiful leather purse. Incredible! I looked for the name of the sender. It was the teacher, the address simply "California," where she had moved.

Our dinner that night was the most delicious I had ever eaten, I could only pray in myself, "Thank you, Father." I forgot I had no money for the rent and only fifteen dollars in my purse and no job. My child and I ate and laughed together in happiness. Then we decorated the little tree and marveled at it. I put Peggy to bed and set up her gifts around the tree, and a sweet peace flooded me like a benediction. I had some hope again. I could even examine the sheaf of bills without cringing. Then I opened the two white envelopes. One contained a check for thirty dollars from a company I had worked for briefly in the summer. It was, said a note, my "Christmas bonus." My rent!

The other envelope was an offer of a permanent position with the government—to begin two days after Christmas. I sat with the letter in my hand and the check on the table before me, and I think that was the most joyful moment of my life up to that time.

The church bells began to ring. I hurriedly looked at my child, who was sleeping blissfully, and ran down to the street. Everywhere people were walking to church to celebrate the birth of the Savior. People smiled at me and I smiled back. The storm had stopped, the sky was pure and glittering with stars.

"The Lord is born!" sang the bells to the crystal night and the laughing darkness. Someone began to sing, "Come, all ye faithful!" I joined in and sang with the strangers all about me.

I am not alone at all, I thought. I was never alone at all.

And that, of course, is the message of Christmas. We are never alone. Not when the night is darkest, the wind coldest, the world seemingly most indifferent. For this is still the time God chooses.

*Taylor Caldwell*

# Away in a Manger

MARTIN LUTHER

GERMAN
Arranged by R. H.

*Tenderly*

1. A - way in a man - ger, no crib for His
2. The cat - tle are low - ing, the poor Ba - by

Loo, loo, loo, loo, loo, loo,

bed, The lit - tle Lord Je - sus laid down His sweet
wakes, But lit - tle Lord Je - sus, no cry - ing He

loo, Loo, loo,— loo, loo, loo, loo, loo,

head. The stars in the sky,— looked down where He
makes; I love Thee, Lord Je - sus, look down from the

loo, Loo, loo, loo, loo, loo, loo, loo,

lay, The lit - tle Lord Je - sus a - sleep in the hay.
sky, And stay by my cra - dle till morn - ing is nigh.

loo, Loo, loo, loo, loo,— loo, Loo,— loo, loo.

The Reflections of

*Christmas*

# Christmas

Christmas and heaven both live in the heart;
May the light of the Bethlehem star
Shine down clear and bright,
    through the darkness of night,
And bless you wherever you are.

Each day's rosy dawning, and red rising sun,
And through the long hours to come,
May the spirit which makes
    this Christmas so warm,
Multiply to a fabulous sum.

May love and good fortune be yours every hour,
And a spirit of faith that will sing,
To lift up your soul redeemed
    and made whole,
Like the music of bubbling springs.

*Dan A. Hoover*

# This Time of Year

When Christmas carols have been stilled
And gifts are no longer new,
Will we keep Christmas in our hearts
With all the joys we knew?

Long after shepherds have gone back
To watching o'er their sheep,
Will we remember all year long
Peace and goodwill to keep?

Why have the Christmas spirit stay
For just one day a year,
When we could easily each day
Create goodwill and cheer?

Let's keep that one star shining bright
As it did long ago . . .
By keeping love within our hearts
We keep his light aglow.

*Carice Williams*

# The Day That Follows Christmas

On the day that follows Christmas
When the house is strangely still,
When the push and rush are over
I enjoy a special thrill.

All the happy preparations
Are still evident around
In the vivid decorations,
In the goodies that abound.

Now there's time to read the letters
I had scanned so hurriedly;
Time to sort the cards so festive
With their greetings warming me.

Poignantly, the Christmas story
And its message, clear and low,
Seem to pierce the heart more deeply
In this quiet afterglow.

*Louise A. Baldwin*

*Photo opposite*
*Tony Stone Assoc., Ltd.*

# Christmas Legends

Christmas morn, the legends say,
Even the cattle kneel to pray,
Even the beasts of wood and field
Homage to Christ the Savior yield.
Horse and cow and woolly sheep
Wake themselves from their heavy sleep,
Bending heads and knees to him
Who came to earth in a stable dim.
Faraway in the forest dark
Creatures timidly wake and hark.
Feathered bird and furry beast
Turn their eyes to the mystic east.
Loud at the dawning, chanticleer
Sounds his note, the rest of the year,
But Christmas Eve the whole night long
Honoring Christ he sings his song.
Christmas morn, the legends say,
Even the cattle kneel to pray,
Even the wildest beast afar
Knows the light of the Savior's star.

*Denis A. McCarthy*

# "Read to Me"

## The Animals at Christmas

Of all the beautiful stories and legends of the Christmas season, there's one that I love the best and which became a tradition to my legion of radio listeners. It is the story about the animals who were given the power to speak on Christmas Eve, so that they could remind each other of the shelter their kind once gave the Infant Jesus, who was born in a stable and cradled in a manger because there was no room at the Inn of Bethlehem. Time passed, and the Star of Bethlehem grew dim in their short memories, and finally the last of the animals who had been in the stable on that memorable Christmas Eve died. Who knows, perhaps in some poor stable even now, an ox kneels in reverence at midnight and whispers to his neighbor. Somehow I'm afraid the animals have all forgotten the manger in Bethlehem and the story that was given them to tell. Here is the story that begins . . . not once upon a time, but, upon a midnight clear . . .

They say there is among us a place where children and young animals play together so their hearts are one. And in this place on Christmas Eve, the power of speech came to some young creatures: a calf, a donkey, and a baby lamb. The calf knelt upon its slender knees and then spoke, saying, "I kneel, yet I do not know exactly why. There was a child last summer who patted my head and whispered in my ear. I remember the child . . . was it a manger it whispered about? A stable?" The other young animals made no answer, and then the donkey spoke, "I, too, remember a child, a child who pointed to the shadow of a cross on my back. It makes me think of a story . . . about a journey to a distant land and the burden on my back. But I cannot remember exactly." Then the baby lamb stirred softly and asked, "Does the story tell of a still night and a bright star in the east? There was such a night. I almost remember."

For a time they were silent, struggling to recall the things only half-remembered, yet they felt that somehow a child was a part of the story. If they only knew how to put them all together, then the fragments of their dreams would be made whole. The manger, the stable, the long journey on a still night, and the bright star in the east. But only a child could help them tell the story of the old, old mystery. And suddenly there was with them a child, and a great light shone around him—a child in swaddling clothes, as in the manger so long ago, and yet not unlike the children of the summer just past. He spoke . . . and as they listened their dreams were made whole, and the young animals once again remembered the Christmas story. And once again, as we approach the Christmas season, the prayer in all our hearts is that the star that guided those wise men will sometime shine upon a world where there is really peace on earth, goodwill to all mankind.

*Lorraine Sherwood*

# May You Know Joy

May you, wherever you are in this golden hour, know joy. May your hearth fire be surrounded with those near and dear to you; the happiness of your children reecho the gladness heaven sends forth in this time of the miracle of Bethlehem.

May the faith the humble shepherds found in the starlit stable be yours in fullest measure; the exultation of Mary and Joseph light your heart with the glow of divine love.

May you gather together in bright bouquet love, charity and tranquility of spirit, for he who possesses these holds the key to riches beyond measure.

May all your dreams in this splendid hour reach fulfillment, and may all the paths you walk be lighted with peace, not only today, but in all the days of the year to come.

*Loretta Bauer Buckley*

# CHRISTMAS

I'm thinking of Christmas as it was years ago;
To be really perfect there had to be snow.
We'd set up the manger that Mother had made,
Then help with the tree while the phonograph played.
The house would be dusted and polished and clean,
And cards were displayed where each could be seen.
Our mother's big kitchen would smell extra nice;
For days she'd been busy with sugar and spice.
The wind-up train waited upon its small track
For Christmas additions from Santa's big pack.
We'd get up really early while street lights were on,
For the spirit of Christmas seemed closer at dawn.
We'd look in our stockings for trinkets and treats,
Then open our presents all wrapped up so neat.

By the front parlor window where it could be seen,
Our tree would be standing so splendid and green.
There were garlands of tinsel and bright paper chains,
Some small shining bells and peppermint canes.
Some twisted wax candles were clipped on the tree;
They seldom were lighted but pretty to see.
Our time-honored angel would be in its place
And frosty glass Santa there swinging in space.
The icicles shimmered on twigs here and there,
And the pretty glass fish swam high in the air.
The lights were reflected in each colored ball,
And a big golden star shone high above all.

# MEMORIES

Beneath the low branches a tiny farm grew—
With buildings and people and animals, too.
Small fences and meadows, a road and some trees,
With lakes made of mirrors and boats upon these.
Some celluloid ducklings, a deer and some does,
With penny-doll people in tiniest clothes.
A woodpile and wagons and little toy cars,
A pump and a lantern for this farm of ours.
Some years it was winter with white cotton snow,
And others were summer with green things to show.
All made and arranged by our mother each year
With extra surprises when Christmas was here.

When church bells were ringing, we went down the hill
To church for a service of peace and goodwill.
If Christmas was Sunday, a program was due,
With children all singing and piece-speaking too.
Or sometimes a pageant with costumes and all,
Some angels and shepherds and a star on the wall.
So nice walking homeward in new-fallen snow,
To call Merry Christmas to people we'd know
And to hear jingling bells on each passing sleigh—
Our hearts filled with gladness for such a fine day.
Christmas in those days was simple you see
But fond recollections endear it to me.

*Harriet Whipple*

# Reflections at Winter Twilight

Ah, the crunch beneath my feet affords me certain delight as I inhale the pine against the frosty air. It seems to cleanse and soothe the battered lungs. My breath crystallizes and ascends in cotton puffs at rhythmic intervals, spelling out an unknown code that stories my inner soul. The higher I climb, the more intense the sanctum becomes. I do feel his presence and his pulse throbs within my heart.

A gentle wind swirls the powdery snow into my reddened face, and yet another sense is awakened. Standing now at the summit amidst the fading light, I see a shroud of dusk permeating the silent hills, enveloping all but the peaks of the sentinel firs. And there upon the endless horizon an explosion of colors rises and falls within the kaleidoscope sky—at first a gentle blue streaked with gilding—lacy wisps about the heavens. Then gold gives way to peach, and peach to scarlet—this panorama leaves me agape! For here my God silently work his miracles, testament to his existence.

Yet in my world so many rebuke him, so many doubt him. What more proof do they need? They deny him through reason and science, and ignore his wonders and call them chemistry. How sad they are!

Here on my precipice it has grown dark, yet he has not forgotten me. For even now in this cavern of night, he gives me moonlight to see and stars to guide me—down the crunching slope past the sentinel firs and swirling snow—back to my loved ones, by the brick hearth, and its crackling embers.

I shall not forget these solitary feelings. I will carry with me the message of joy and feelings of hope, that one day I will join him in the place where he creates these miracles.

*Timothy Traynor*

# Memories
# of a
# Country Christmas

Before the turn of the century, I remember, the first sign that Christmas was getting near was the night we had bowls of beef broth and crackers for supper. It never happened at any other time of year.

The reason was that my mother had bought a piece of beef and had it simmering on the back of the coal-burning living room stove all day. It was seasoned with salt and pepper but no onions because of the beef's ultimate destiny.

This was the foundation for the holiday mincemeat pie.

Next day came the chopping, not grinding; there was no meat grinder. Each kind of ingredient was put into the big, old, wooden chopping bowl and attacked with the steel chopping knife until it was reduced to fine pieces. As my mother chopped the meat and apples and raisins, I always asked to help. But small arms were soon tired and always glad to relinquish the job to her.

Mother added spices, sugar, molasses, jelly, cider, raisins and currants, and I remember saying to her once, "You don't need a rule for this; you just put in a little of everything you have in the house."

She said, "Well, not quite, but when you have one third meat and two thirds apple, you can sort of

play it by ear after that."

All that day the wonderful smells sifted through the house. By evening, after many stirrings and tastings, the whole kettleful was transferred to a big stone crock, then covered and set in the "cold pantry" to ripen the flavors for the holidays.

Usually we did not have a Christmas tree; the filled stockings hung the evening before were our highlight. There was the orange in the stocking toe, some fruit and candy, small toys and books, always colored crayons. When I was five there was a big doll from my grandmother; the year after came a high chair for her to sit in. This was the only big doll I ever had, but it was enough. Her name was Dorothy and she lasted as long as I played with dolls. Some of my sewing lessons went into making her clothes and patchwork bed quilts.

One year we went to another grandmother's house, and there we really had a wonderful Christmas tree. It was a long drive from our house, about twenty miles, and that's a long trip with a horse and sleigh. The sleigh bells went jingle-jangle and we were tucked in snugly under a big, old buffalo robe. The grandparents had eight children and each of them had several children. Each family lived in a different town so we all went a day ahead. There must have been at least thirty people there, maybe more.

For supper Grandmother made a whopping clam chowder in the washboiler and we had big "common" crackers, the kind that split in the middle, to go with it. Grandmother made her own butter so that chowder was wonderfully rich. We had Indian pudding and cream for dessert that night. The long row of pies on the pantry shelf were for the big feast the next day.

After supper, the women cleaned up the kitchen and the men settled down in the living room to talk. How I loved to sit quietly in some corner and listen. Since they came from different places, each told of the funniest and most interesting things that had happened during the past year. We could learn a lot by just keeping still.

When it was time for bed, I remember that four of us small girl cousins slept crosswise in a big bed, sinking deep into the featherbed with many giggles and finding it hard to get to sleep.

For breakfast next morning, there were big iron skillets full of country fried potatoes, pancakes, and eggs. Then the children were shooed out of the kitchen while the women cooked the biggest turkey they had been able to find, and heaps of vegetables of all kinds. The row of pies included squash and mince and apple. We had brought our mincemeat.

All this time no child had been allowed in the parlor, whose door was shut tight. After the big dinner, we still had to wait until the dishes were washed, dried, and put away. It seemed like forever.

Finally the last hands were dried, the last aprons whisked off and hung up. Then the door opened into fairyland. A hemlock tree touched the ceiling. It was shining in beauty, and better yet, loaded with gifts. The small gifts were tied on branches; the heavier ones were piled on the floor beneath.

Grandfather passed out the presents. He made a good Santa Claus because he had a white beard anyway, so he didn't need a mask. He also had a jolly smile most of the time so he was suited to this task by nature. These are some of my memories of a country Christmas . . . long, long ago.

*Hazel Andrews*

# Ring on,
# O Happy Bells

Ring on, O bells of gladness
With your message of good cheer;
Peal forth the merry tidings
In cadence sweet and clear.

Ring out the old year fading,
With its failures, let it go;
Ring in the joy and promise
Of a new year's rosy glow.

Chime forth your skyborne music,
With its intervals of mirth;
Arouse the aspirations
And hopes of all the earth.

Ring on, O bells of gladness,
With the joy you now impart;
Ring on and on, O happy bells,
And bring a song to every heart.

*Joy Belle Burgess*

# Stopping by Woods on a Snowy Evening

Whose woods these are I think I know.
His house is in the village, though;
He will not see me stopping here
To watch his woods fill up with snow.

My little horse must think it queer
To stop without a farmhouse near
Between the woods and frozen lake
The darkest evening of the year.

He gives his harness bells a shake
To ask if there is some mistake.
The only other sound's the sweep
Of easy wind and downy flake.

The woods are lovely, dark, and deep,
But I have promises to keep,
And miles to go before I sleep,
And miles to go before I sleep.

*Robert Frost*